THE AWKWARD SILENCE

THE AWKWARD SILENCE

Poems by W. D. Ehrhart

NORTHWOODS PRESS, INC.

Library of Congress Catalog Card No.: 79 92943

ISBN No. 0-89002-133-3, Paper
ISBN No. 0-89002-134-1, Cloth

This book is #5 of the Northwoods Special Poetry Project-an ongoing series of 64 page poetry books written to a theme by the best poets we can find.

NORTHWOODS PRESS, INC.
PO Box 249
Stafford, VA 22554

Some of these poems have previously appeared in *American Report, Aspect, The Daily Intelligencer, DEMILITARIZED ZONES, Driftwood East, FRONT LINES, Glamour, In These Times, LISTEN: THE WAR, Midwest, The News-Herald, Perspective, THE PILLORY POETICS, Place, Samisdat, Scribe, Shantih, Student Lawyer, Svetova Literatura, Trends, WELCOM IN ZONNIG SAIGON, Win, Wind, and WINNING HEARTS AND MINDS;* also in *A GENERATION OF PEACE* from New Voices, and *A GENERATION OF PEACE, ROOTLESS, EMPIRE* from Samisdat Press.

For Merritt Clifton and June Kemp,
and for Jan Barry

CONTENTS

I

WINNING HEARTS AND MINDS

ONE NIGHT ON GUARD DUTY

The first salvo is gone before I can turn,
but there is still time to see the cannons
hurl a second wave of steel against the dark.

The shells arc up,
tearing through the air like some invisible hand
crinkling giant sheets of cellophane among the stars.

The night waits, breathless,
till the far horizon erupts in brilliant
pulsing silence.

SOUVENIRS

"Bring me back a souvenir," the captain called.
"Sure thing," I shouted back above the Amtrac's roar.

Later that day,
the column halted,
we found a Buddhist temple by the trail.
Combing through a nearby woods,
we found a heavy log as well.

It must have taken more than half an hour;
but at last we battered in
the concrete walls so badly
that the roof collapsed.

Before it did,
I took two painted vases
Buddhists use for burning incense.

One vase I kept,
and one I offered proudly to the captain.

FARMER NGUYEN

When we swept through farmer Nguyen's hamlet,
some people said that farmer Nguyen
had given rice to the Vietcong.

    You picked the wrong side, farmer Nguyen.
    We took you in, and beat you
    and put you in a barbed wire cage.

When the Vietcong returned to farmer Nguyen's hamlet,
some people said that farmer Nguyen
had given information to the Yankees.

    Wrong again, farmer Nguyen.
    They took more rice, and beat you,
    and made you carry supplies.

SERGEANT JONES

And then there's Sergeant Jones.
He's hard, but knows the ways
to handle other men
when they're afraid.

Always has a good word, too.
Not just for us either--
speaks Vietnamese fluently;
makes the girls at the district office
giggle with delight
every time we go there.

The kind of guy the young enlisted men
admire:
he can hit a gook at 50 yards
with a fuckin' .45.

THE RAT

Flashing jagged teeth,
he squealed and shrieked and tried
to break the circle of our flailing rifle butts.

But he couldn't, and at last,
trapped in a corner of the bunker,
he only glared at us through wild
uncomprehending eyes.

His final glimpse of life
was the bottom of a cinderblock.

THE SNIPER'S MARK

He seemed in a curious hurry
to burn up what was left
of the energy inside--

A brainless, savage flurry
of arms and legs and eyes.

MAIL CALL

It's strange, the obstacles
that fail to break the will:
boredom, body rot, pervasive fear of death.
Stranger still, the unanticipated breath
that tips the scales:

            Private Thomas married
only weeks before he left. Now, ten months past,
he was our point man--unscathed, unharried,
though constantly exposed. Ten months unmarked--

and over in an instant with a single shot
that punched a hole in the hot day; with Thomas,
lifeless, sprawled across his cot;
with the lawyer's note,
blood-spattered, crumpled in his fist:
with his last "I love you" trapped inside his throat
by the barrel of a pistol.

THE ONE THAT DIED

You bet we'll soon forget the one that died;
he isn't welcome anymore.
He could too easily take our place
for us to think about him
any longer than it takes
to sort his personal effects:
    a pack of letters,
    some cigarettes,
    photos and a wallet.
We'll keep the cigarettes;
divide them up among us.
His parents have no use for them,
and cigarettes are hard to get.

PERIMETER GUARD

Crouched in a corner,
shivering, damp,
Gerry asleep beside me,
I stand the last
two-hour watch
of a long, tired night.
To the east,
the stars are fading:
grey appears;
then pink, red, and blue.

THE BOB HOPE CHRISTMAS SPECIAL

They went to Cam Ranh Bay,
to Saigon, and Danang--
to anywhere that was secure,
and had good roads, and showers.

They made the headlines
with their down-home girls
and dedication to the boys.

They never got to where the fighting was,
to where the face of yesterday
looked exactly like tomorrow.

They never gave a show for those
who found relief in cigarettes,
dry socks, and no patrol today.

In thirteen months,
I never saw the USO.
But once in August, near Hoi An,
Floyd Patterson shook my hand.

NIGHT PATROL

Another night coats the nose and ears:
smells of fish and paddy water,
smoke from cooking fires and stale urine
drift uneasily, cloaked in silence;
the marketplace deserted, shuttered
houses, empty paths, all cloaked in silence;
shadows bristle.

Our gravel-crunching boots tear great
holes in the darkness, make us wince
with every step. A mangy dog
pits the stomach; rifles level,
nervous fingers hit the safety catch.

THE NEXT STEP

The next step you take
may lead you into an ambush.

The next step you take
may hit a wall of rocket-fire.

The next step you take
may detonate a mine.

The next step you take
may tear your leg off at the hip.

The next step you take
may split your belly open.

The next step you take
may send a sniper's bullet through your brain.

The next step you take.
The next step you take.

The next step.
The next step.

The next step.

GUERRILLA WAR

It's practically impossible
to tell civilians
from the Vietcong.

Nobody wears uniforms.
They all talk
the same language,
(and you couldn't understand them
even if they didn't).

They tape grenades
inside their clothes,
and carry satchel charges
in their market baskets.

Even their women fight;
and young boys,
and girls.

It's practically impossible
to tell civilians
from the Vietcong;

after awhile,
you quit trying.

TIME ON TARGET

We used to get intelligence reports
from the Vietnamese district offices.
Every night, I'd make a list
of targets for artillery to hit.

It used to give me quite a kick
to know that I, a corporal,
could command an entire battery
to fire anywhere I said.

One day, while on patrol,
we passed the ruins of a house;
beside it sat a woman
with her left hand torn away;
beside her lay a child, dead.

When I got back to base,
I told the fellows in the COC;
it gave us all a lift to know
all those shells we fired every night
were hitting something.

HUNTING

Sighting down the long black barrel,
I wait till front and rear sights
form a perfect line on his body,
then slowly squeeze the trigger.

The thought occurs
that I have never hunted anything in my whole life
except other men.

But I have learned by now
where such thoughts lead.
My mind soon passes on
to chow, and sleep,
and how much longer till I change my socks.

CHRIST

I saw the Crucified Christ three days ago.
He did not hang on the cross,
but lay instead on the shambled terrace
of what had been a house.
There were no nails in His limbs,
no crown of thorns, no open wounds.
The soldiers had left nothing
but a small black hole upon His cheek.
And He did not cry: ''Forgive them, Lord;''
but only lay there, gazing at an ashen sky.

Today, on the Rusurrection,
angelic hosts of flies caress His brow;
and from His swollen body comes
the sweet-sick stench of rotting flesh.

THE HAWK AND TWO SUNS

The silver hawk swoops 300 miles per hour
almost standing still,
locks his grid-coordinate prey
between his cross-haired eyes,
holds, extends twin silver talons--
cannisters that tumble through the air--
almost horizontal, they strike the ground together.

Coming from the sun, the hawk creates another sun
that spreads a brilliant orange sun-storm
that billows out and rolls along the earth;
billows, then recedes;
leaves behind burnt-black bodies and lungs
burst outward in frantic search of oxygen.

The hawk shrieks his predatory victory cry
and wheels away to join the greater sun
he drains with every raid.

THE GENERALS' WAR

Paper orders passed down and executed:

straggling back in plum-colored rags,
one-legged, in slings, on stretchers,
in green plastic bags,
with stubbled faces
and gaunt eyes hung in sockets;

returned to paper
for some general to read about
and pin a medal to.

THE AMBUSH

Illusion:
waiting come to an end.

The target:
black shape
against the bluer black of night.

Response:
extremities converge inside the chest,
burst outward through the arms,
explode
from the muzzle of an automatic rifle
toward the lurching, speechless figure
caught mid-sentence
by the fury of an inability to hate.

> (The target is a pretext;
> it has a hundred names.
> None belong to it;
> all are out of reach.)

Respite:
through the long night after,
sleep--the deep and total sleep
that swallows one whose mind is without thought,
empty, drained, at peace.

Illusion shattered:
daylight;
things remain as they were.

ANOTHER LIFE

The long day's march is over.
Ten thousand meters through the bush
with flak jacket, rifle, helmet,
three hundred rounds of ammunition,
three days' rations, two canteens,
hand grenades, a cartridge belt;
pack straps grinding at the shoulders,
feet stuffed in boots that stumble forward
mile after hill after hour;
the sun a crushing hundred-and-two,
sweat in the eyes and salt on the lips;
and always aware that Charlie only waits.

The march is over for today.
Now, heaped against a paddy dike
and fighting back the sweetness of exhaustion,
I close my eyes
and struggle to recall
another life.

COMING HOME

San Francisco airport--

no more corpsmen stuffing ruptured chests
with cotton balls and not enough heat tabs
to eat a decent meal.

I asked some girl to sit
and have a Coke with me.
She thought I was crazy;
I thought she was going to call a cop.

I bought a ticket for Philadelphia.
At the loading gate, they told me:
"Thank you for flying TWA;
we hope you will enjoy your flight."

No brass bands;
no flags,
no girls,
no cameramen.

Only a small boy who asked me
what the ribbons on my jacket meant.

II

DEMILITARIZED ZONES

IMAGINE

The conversation turned Vietnam.
He'd been there, and they asked him
what it had been like:
had he been in battle?
Had he ever been afraid?

Patiently, he tried to answer
questions he had tried to answer
many times before.

They listened, and they strained
to visualize the words:
newsreels and photographs, books
and Wilfred Owen tumbled
through their minds.
Pulses quickened.

They didn't notice, as he talked,
his eyes, as he talked,
his eyes begin to focus
through the wall, at nothing,
or at something inside.

When he finished speaking,
someone asked him:
had he ever killed?

DANCING

Having been where contrasts meet,
I perceive reality to be
whatever looms largest in the mind.

Thus, truths are never absolute;
nebulous, they never lose the shifting
beat of music changing time:

books I read, and faces seen
in sunlight tell me where I am.
At night, this truth slips away;

an older truth looms within
and I submit, take my rifle,
rejoin comrades on patrol

until the sun returns the books,
and faces, and the other truth
I dance with to a kinder beat.

OLD MYTHS

Citations, medals, warrants of promotion:

all the things I ever earned I framed
and tacked up in the attic room
I used to use for studying.

That was many years ago--
before events began to show
how deeply they were etched.

Now the room is cluttered with old clothes
and broken toys and boxes.
I don't go up there anymore;
I've lived the myth, and know it
for a lie.

Yet even now, sometimes I find
traces of an older pride:

I guess old myths die hard.

A RELATIVE THING

We are the ones you sent to fight a war
you didn't know a thing about.

It didn't take us long to realize
the only land that we controlled
was covered by the bottoms of our boots.

When the newsmen said that naval ships
had shelled a VC staging point,
we saw a breastless woman
and her stillborn child.

We laughed at old men stumbling
in the dust in frenzied terror
to avoid our three-ton trucks.

We fought outnumbered in Hue City
while the ARVN soldiers looted bodies
in the safety of the rear.
The cookies from the wives of Local 104
did not soften our awareness.

We have seen the pacified supporters
of the Saigon government
sitting in their jampacked cardboard towns,
their wasted hands placed limply in their laps,
their empty bellies waiting for the rice
some district chief has sold
for profit to the Vietcong.

We have seen Democracy on Zippo raids,
burning hooches to the ground,
driving eager amtracs through a farmer's fields.

We are the ones who have to live
with the memory that we were the instruments
of your pigeon-breasted fantasies.
We are inextricable accomplices
in this travesty of dreams:
but we are not alone.

We are the ones you sent to fight a war
you did not know a thing about--
those of us who lived
have tried to tell you what went wrong.
Now you think you do not have to listen.

Just because we will not fit
into the uniforms of photographs
of you at twenty-one
does not mean you can disown us.

We are your sons, America,
and you cannot change that.
When you awake
we will still be here.

TO THE ASIAN VICTORS

The great miscalculation
refuses to be covered over.
I have tried every solution,
yet the paint always begins to peel
even before it is dry,
and the bare room comes back
again.

This last time
it returned as yellow frightened faces
spilling from the bellies of birds,
like splinters from old wounds
that will not heal.

In school, as a child,
I learned about Redcoats--
I studied myself,
though I did not know it at the time.
The lesson remains;
only the teacher has changed.

Looking back
at the pale shadow forever
calling at dusk from the forest,
I remember the dead, I
remember the dying.

But I cannot ever quite remember
what I went looking for,
or what it was I lost
in that alien land that became
more I
than my own can ever be again.

TO MAYNARD ON THE LONG ROAD HOME

Biking at night with no lights
and no helmet, you were struck
and hurled sixty feet,
dead on impact.
The newspapers noted the irony:
surviving the war
to die like that, alone,
on a hometown street.
I knew better.

Years before, on Christmas Day,
I met you on a road near Quang Tri;
a chance reunion of Perkasie boys
grown up together in a town
that feared God and raised sons
willing to die for their country.
''Who're you with?
Have you seen much action?
What the hell's going on here?''
All that afternoon we remembered
our shared youth: the old boat
with Jeffy and the slow leak,
skipping Sunday School to read comics
and drink orange soda at Flexer's,
the covered bridge near Bryan's farm.
Though neither of us
spoke of it, we knew then
we had lost
more than our youth.

I show my poems to friends now and then,
hoping one or two might see
my idealistic bombast
in a new light:
the sharp turns of mood, anger
defying visible foundation,
inexplicable sadness.
How often they wonder aloud
how I managed to survive--
they always assume the war is over,
not daring to imagine our wounds,
or theirs, if it is not.
I think of you, my friend,
and wonder if either of us
will ever make it home.

MAKING THE CHILDREN BEHAVE

Do they think of me now
in those strange Asian villages
where nothing ever seemed
quite human
but myself
and my few green friends
moving through them
hunched
in lines?

When they tell stories to their children
of the evil
that awaits misbehavior,
is it me they conjure?

LETTER

to a North Vietnamese soldier
whose life crossed paths with mine
in Hue, February 5th, 1968

Thought you killed me
with that rocket? Well you nearly did:
splattered walls and splintered air,
knocked me cold and full of holes,
and brought the roof down on my head.

But I lived,
long enough to wonder often
how you missed; long enough
to wish too many times
you hadn't.

What's it like back there?
It's all behind us here;
and after all those years of possibility,
things are back to normal.
We just had a special birthday,
and we've found again our inspiration
by recalling where we came from
and forgetting where we've been.

Oh, we're still haggling over pieces
of the lives sticking out
beyond the margins of our latest
history books; but no one haggles
with the authors.

Do better than that
you cockeyed gunner with the brass
to send me back alive among a people
I can never feel
at ease with anymore:

remember where you've been, and why.
And then build houses;
build villages, songs and children,
dikes and schools; build
communion in that green land
I blackened with my shadow
and the shadow of my flag.

Remember Ho Chi Minh
was a poet: please,
do not let it all
come down to nothing.

VIETNAMESE-CAMBODIAN BORDER WAR

January 1978

Stories on the six o'clock news;
familiar diagrams:
the Parrot's Beak, a black
arrow pointing west. ''The same
route taken by U.S. soldiers...''
(May, 1970)--
poker-faced, the newscasters
never fail to mention
the connection.

Like these years of silence,
the reminder too
is deliberate:
the Communists
are fighting each other now.

America quietly smirks;
orders another drink.

A CONFIRMATION

for Gerry Gaffney,
a good friend in a bad time

Solemn Douglas firs stride slowly
down steep hills to drink
the waters of the wild Upper Umqua.
In a small clearing in the small
carved ravine of a feeder stream
we camp, pitching our tent
in the perfect stillness of the shadows
of the Klamath Indians. Far off
almost in a dream, the logging trucks
growl west down through the mountains
toward the mills in Roseburg.

I hold the stakes, you hammer--
''Watch the fingers!''--both laughing.
Both recall, in easy conversation,
one-man poncho tents rigged
side by side in total darkness;
always you and I, in iron heat,
in the iron monsoon rains--
not like this at all; and yet,
though years have passed
and we are older by a lifetime,
a simple slip of thought, a pause,
and here: nothing's changed.

For we were never young, it seems:
not then, or ever. I couldn't even cry
the day you went down, screaming, jagged
angry steel imbedded in your knee--
I knew you would live,
and I knew you wouldn't be back,
and I was glad, and a little jealous.
Two months later I went down.

We all went down eventually,
the villages aflame, the long
grim lines of soldiers, flotsam
in the vortex of a sinking illusion:
good-bye, Ginny; good-bye, John Kennedy;
good-bye, Tom Paine and high school history--
though here we are still, you and I.
We live our lives now
in a kind of awkward silence
in the perfect stillness of the shadows
of the Klamath Indians.

And I am genuinely happy
to be with you again. We stand
on the rocks; you point to clear
patches between white water
where the shadows of sleek fish slip,
effortless streaks of energy.
I'm clumsy: with an old, eager patience
you teach me how to cast the fly
gently, so it rides on the surface
with the current, far downstream--
till the rod bends, springs back,

bends again: strike! Your excitement
rises above the river like a wild
song the Douglas firs bend
imperceptibly to hear: shouts,
advice, encouragement, half an hour
and a fourteen-inch rainbow trout
panting hard, eyes alive, its tiny heart
beating with defiance still unbroken
though I hold the fish
helpless in my hands.

I throw the fish back
in the awkward silence, and you
slip your arm around my shoulders
gently for a moment, knowing why.

Later we eat from cans,
the rainbow flashing in the fire
reflecting in our eyes, alive:
familiar gestures--fingers burned
by hot tin lids, a mild curse, quiet
laughter, swish of a knifeblade
plunging idly deep into damp earth.
You ask do I remember the little shy
flower who always wore a white Ao Dai,
and I smile across the flames as the river
tumbles through the darkness toward the sea
that laps the shores of Asia.

The wind moves through the Douglas firs,
and in the perfect stillness of the shadows
of the Klamath Indians, we test

our bonds and find them, after all
these years, still sound--knowing
in the awkward silence we will always share
something worth clinging to
out of the permanent past of stillborn dreams:
the ancient, implacable wisdom
of ignorance shattered forever, a new
reverence we were never taught
by anyone we believed, a frail hope
we gave each other, communion
made holy by our shame.

You've found religion since then,
a wife, and two children;
I write poems you admire.
The knee's still stiff, like an old
high school football wound,
and I have trouble hearing. We are
both tired, but reluctant to sleep:
both understand we will never
see each other again; once is enough.
The logging trucks have long since
left the mountains in peace;
in the perfect stillness, we can almost
hear the solemn Douglas firs drinking
the waters of the wild Upper Umqua
we have come so far to worship:
together now, in this small circle of light,
we bow our hearts to the shadows
of the Klamath Indians; now--
and always--in our need.

TO THOSE WHO HAVE GONE HOME TIRED

After the streets fall silent
After the bruises and the tear-gassed eyes are healed
After the concensus has returned
After the memories of Kent and My Lai and Hiroshima
lose their power
and their connections with each other
and the sweaters labeled Made In Taiwan
After the last American dies in Canada
and the last Korean in prison
and the last Indian at Pine Ridge
After the last whale is emptied from the sea
and the last leopard emptied from its skin
and the last drop of blood refined by Exxon
After the last iron door clangs shut
behind the last conscience
and the last loaf of bread is hammered into bullets
and the bullets
scattered among the hungry

What answers will you find
What armor will protect you
when your children ask you

Why?